Fragmented Reality

Free The Vision

Copyright © 2017 Free The Vision

All rights reserved.

ISBN: 150869592X
ISBN-13: 978-1508695929

DEDICATION

I dedicate this book to the "how". The how will I do it, and what if I can't. The how will this work, and is it even worth it. I dedicate this book to the "why". The why am I doing this, and why is it necessary. The why now, and why try. I have worked on this piece for much longer than I would like to admit, and now as I have completed it, I offer it to others as guidance through their own figuring it out moments. I dedicate this to the achievement of completion, and to those who encouraged me at every fragment of my life from family to friends and the Divine hand that lead me.

WARNING:

BEYOND THIS POINT SHIT CAN GET DEEP

SWIM OR GRAB A LIFE JACKET.

ACKNOWLEDGMENTS

Thank you to everyone who made the book possible. To my family for their direct and indirect investments in this project. Thank you to the people who I shared these experiences with, for better or for the lessons learned. Thank you to the resources that made a project like this possible. Most importantly, thank you to God for loving me through it all.

Free The Vision

This is the insight of Free The Vision...

GOD GAVE ME A PEN

For my pain and my confusion
For my lies and illusions
God gave me a pen.
For my imagination and relations
For my inception and progression
God gave me a pen.
For my understanding and commanding
For my wisdom and insanity
God gave me a pen.
For my love and my trust
For my filthy and yearning lust
God gave me a pen.
For my roots and my truth
For my growth and love of youth
God gave me a pen.
For my prayers and my layers
For my vision and my internal soothsayer
God gave me a pen.
For my wins and my losses
For my concern and my causes
God gave me a pen.
For my history and my endeavors
For all of the treasures of the Divine unmeasured
I thank you God for this pen.
I sign it here, loud and clear...
You are the ink of this pen.

SILENCE

Silence how you speak to me
Such profound words need not be said.
Loud echoes of truth although voicelessly expressed.
Acknowledging these thoughts in my head.
Why must I think them when I try to rest.
Silence should help me relieve
    But silence you taunt my abilities
    I thought we were alone in this darkness
    How can you be so harsh when I'm not fighting.
Silence you take advantage of me.
Not even the blare of the TV can shield me.
Silence say what you must, but be worthy of my trust.
Silence don't misguide me.
Until sleep intoxicates me, silence I welcome thee.

LIVING ON...

You're a walking memory
You own nothing here
Every illusion you experience
Will one day disappear
The ones that love you
Have a time stamp
So what can we do to be known past man?
We must create
And I don't mean some digital "social" page
You must open your mouth & express life
You must forge forward and do what's right
You must plan the vision you see in your mind
Until you look up & see it alive

GREATER DISTINCTION

In my greatest weaknesses
You are my unfailing strength
In my deepest fears
You are my undoubted assurance
In my lowest pains
You are my highest gains
In my worst defeats
You are my redirected victory
In all the imperfections of me
You are the perfection I seek
In my dishonorable decisions
You are my saved precision
I be the worst
You be the best
Together I am balanced and blessed

TO BE HUMBLED

We, the human, with all our intelligence find a consistent way to dumb ourselves down. When we strategize for the gain of our own selfish satisfactions, we find ourselves humbled by our own destruction.

This mirror won't lie, and neither will that rebellious voice of reason that we try our best to tune out, rationalize, and moralize. In a room of silence we still hear echoes of truth.

I humbly accept my disappointments that I personally built. I take away the depressing power of them, by growing from them. I admit my faults, and accept them. We, the human, in all our rationalizations still can't beat the inevitable. Although we can prevent the unnecessary.

BREAK IT UP

Break the cycle
Break the news
Tell the niggas
You're being abused

Break the minds
Break the lines
Tomorrow doesn't exist
Now is the time

Break the lies
Break the ties
Stand alone
Then you'll fly

Break the tradition
Break the conditions
Live brand new
Inside your decisions

Break the chains
Break the reins
Destroy this bondage
Lets live again

R.A.N.T. - Hi Dollar Hi Concern

We live in a society that fights for equality by pretending the separate parties are equals. Instead of constructing the laws to equally serve diverse individuals. Equal means the same, and we are not the same. We were never destined to be.

The more we fold into the seams of mediocrity we become a cluster fuck of anonymity. Unknown, indistinctive. This is the life of apathy. If the dollar is high, so is the concern.

AS IT FLEES…

The days grow dark and the nights grow bright
What I didn't know then is right now's light
Watching familiar pack it's bag
I hear a knock of opportunity arriving fast
But in the confliction of transition
Confusion meets understanding
I mourn the departure
And celebrate the arrival
Growth is inevitable to survival
Greeted by the new I look into you
Wondering how long it will stay before
The new must go too.

Growth Lived Through a Mirror

I stared at my feet and recognized them from a moment in my childhood. I remember looking at them in admiration. I remember liking the beauty marks on them, but finding them mysterious. I felt in that moment I, the physical, was the only one who had experienced life from my point of view. I had been here, with me, everywhere I had gone. I had grown without ever recognizing. I fell victim to counting the years without acknowledging the days, hours, or seconds. My feet had grown before my eyes, which means I had grown before the eyes of others. My evolution was lived out through a mirror.

A Measure to Own...

We live in a time that manipulates self improvement.
They exploit insecurities and corrupt greatness with mediocre impurities.
You are not fine just the way you are.
You were meant to grow and shed the skin you've been given.
Don't do what makes you happy...
Do what fulfills you.
What makes you happy is temporary.
What fulfills you will enrich you, and others.
As long as we settle for good, greatness will seem like an elite privilege.
None of us are perfect, this is the plight of man, but all of us are worth the life we've been given and redefined by the life we create.
Everyday is a celebration in route to a mission.
Don't let the hysteria of deception muddy your perception.
This life, this world, this greatness is as much yours as those in control of the nations.
Remember greatness is achieved and then received...be careful whose perspective you believe.

Saint Louis (Ode to Mike)

I need a mass coalition to change the condition
While facing opposition I met a weakened rendition
Of comfort.

Truth felt like a bullet to the head & a body laid dead for hours.
A vision of a people empowered
A system of blatant deception took a bold direction and hid the coward.

We stand holding the hand of a revolution that just can't sit still
A once quiet acceptance turned into
A relentless rejection needing reformation immediately.

Knowledge is the reflection of power but served like poison to the mind of a fool.
We are the brand new. The ones who will one day be remembered by the history of how we handled our current day travesties.

AS IT SEEMS....

If I always felt as good as it seems
If my smile was full of as much peace as it brings
If I was as well together as some believe
If some of my struggles weren't for me
If I was as strong as I've told others to be
If the truth was as clean as what the eye sees
I wouldn't be me

I rent on Earth
The world of temporary.
Temporary happiness
Temporary pain
Temporary loss
Temporary gains
Temporary life
Temporary strains

With an Endless God that knows us by name
I've called You more times than any number invented
Without doubt You kept me lifted.
You allowed me more Grace than measure
You gave me relief with prayers answered
This is no different so hear me out
Don't let any of my weakness bring me down
Don't let self doubt break my dreams
Come on through with joy please
Let realness be a brand for me

Battery Life Legacy

We are so lost in the concept of time we're fighting for hours while rushing the minutes. We watch the clock steal our lives with the intention to do more, but a weakened drive struggles to endure. The world is a paradox: the most connected they've ever been, and yet more disconnected than then.

Think about it. Before the iPlatform WE found ways to get words and ACTIONS amongst one another to boycott for change. Movements were built and change was dealt. Today everyone is in the know on the surface, but they're less aware that the surface even exist. All while mindlessly chanting "there's levels to this shit." And as television dictates reality, life becomes a soap opera. The system of writers has a plot that ends in tragedy. The government shuts down but the fiscal flow is fluid and consistent for the elite.

Logic escapes us like the pursuit of truth; waiting for the bold question that leads to understanding. In this world of pretenders wanting to be recognized by an abundance of "likes", chasing temporary validation like an addiction, we're all hooked to the technological habit. It has sped up our hours filling them with irrelevance and distractions.

If all clocks stopped the world would continue to turn; days would have no distinction and we'd be left to be defined by what we create. We can't let our legacies die when the phone battery does. Remember someone somewhere needs your perspective to understand their next step. Let the phone die while you live your life. Unlike your phone once your life runs out, there is no recharge.

Well Endowed (The Balls)

They ask who the fuck am I to stand here talking all this shit?
Ol' educated nigger with a whole lotta whit
Big ass d*ck
A physical manifestation of ancestral strength.
A man flawed but built to win.

What Am I Gettin' At?

Speak to the blind
The open of minds
People who view life beyond the times.

I trust to fuck up
I praise to get up
I die to live
I work to give
I am often wrong
I always move on
I'm not a nigga
But I understand their song

I do not judge
I am the worst in silence
A brilliant mind
Full of devious confinement
The truth is not nice
Nor is it wrong
What am I gettin at?
Follow along.

If we really knew why would we ask?
I don't know shit
I'm just blowing gas
Words make sense
In broken cadence
Don't expect much
Just take what you get
Create some new shit
I live & exist
At the end of it all I hope to reach bliss.

Free The Vision

We Mustn't

We mustn't play small or else we gain a fraction of nothingness. We mustn't play small as a means of upholding the old out of a fear and laziness of forging a new. It was the old that brought us to destruction while celebrating a complacent point of view. We mustn't play small.

We mustn't play little when we're most deserving of a lot. We mustn't lust our distractions as an excuse to why stopped. We mustn't forget the tracks made by bare and bloody feet, just so we can pray grace over our lives fearlessly.

We mustn't play silent out of fear to offend those who could careless. Silence is acceptance and worn by cowards like a medal upon their breast. We mustn't fail ourselves by not attempting or appeasing those who don't have to live in the repercussions of our history.

It has become a war between silent settlement and endless gain. We're on the edge of decision asking which path are we going to obtain, and now we can win if we unite without delay. We mustn't pretend as if we don't have shit to say

Romantic Bankruptcy

Suffering the woes of being romantically bankrupt.
Having invested my funds in quick returns often regretting the lessons learned.
Yet and still my body yearns while my heart cries...
Disconnect of affection brings about desperate lies, and a convicted life.
Here is the struggle between weakness of flesh & conquering of mind.
I wish they would feel together & left sorrow behind.
When the checks clear & love wants it's return, lust gives an I.O.U. with no concern.
Yet the emptiness is an illusion
That feeling is really the need for more deserved.
So here a conundrum of affairs
Deep sighs & prayers released in the air
In loneliness of this room I hope to find myself fulfilled while contemplating here.

A Victim of Self

Mass murder befalls your vision as the weapons of your past leave stains of your future's blood on your hands. You wash and wash but keep picking up the very dagger that gave you so little life you couldn't face reality. Now confusion honors you like a guest in it's mansion of disillusion, serving you turmoil buffet style. Less we come to give or be it we come to take. Now you're standing in the gap of the shadow & the light. Not realizing it is your light that leaves your shadow behind. Haunted and taunted we lose our peace but a Divine army of angels keep you guarded with a relentless piece. Deep in stillness we find truth, broken by realness we lose youth. And what do we say it to these cadavers? May God give you life and birth from your disaster.

Untitled: 2.14.15

Answers evaded them like light to a cave. They searched. In route to what seemed to be the exit from what had now grown stale, Life introduced them to opposing familiarities. A retake at an overlook.
A mirrored reflection that had become so unrecognizable that its existence felt like a contradiction to all they had known. It wasn't that love had become extinct, but that it had become neglected.
The children of their anger had separated their understanding. Where was the entrance to next for them? A painful conquest that didn't show signs of a finish line. Just then an epiphany walked into the room delivering a message: Next was a continuous evolution of now, so the finish line is hidden behind the creation of a new beginning.

Ellipses

Old habits linger around my thoughts like vultures to the dying. They wait to capitalize on my peace and they leave me feeling a sense of defeat because deep, real deep, I know they're a familiar place to somewhere I no longer want to stay but to leave them is to feel abandoned by my own ways.

Him to He

I became a man before my eyes
But there's a boy inside my mind
That struggles to find the place he once called home.

He said "When did we get all of this?"
I replied, "As we kept living kid."
He says "Damn what a trip."
I say "It's a journey we can't resist"

With a snare he stares and ask:
"So you're the one with all the answers."
But I'm the opposite.
I am the conquistador asking the questions.
He rages for place but he cannot stay.

Dear Words...

Words,

You are such a refuge. I take you to Thee Creator and you're brought back to me in tangibles. You allow me to release myself and all my emotions, confusion, joy, peace, pain, and love. Once you leave me, I am unable to regain you...but there are so many of you that you don't leave me empty.

The pure idea that you, words, are able to move the world into peace or war shows just the significance of you. My beautiful words, I think you're often misunderstood but always used. Some times too often. As a matter of fact, your strength can go unnoticed because of how many people overuse you. Yet, when properly aligned you can rework the mind and for that you are a beautiful channel to life. Words, thank you.

The Hour of Silence

In the hour of silence there is a whispering of truths unfiltered.

We open our ears to hear

Our hearts to receive

Our love to entice

Our spirit to awaken

And our mind to expand.

Thinking: ver. 22:55 - 7/28.15

There's like this punishment that loneliness has. It's called desperation. The pains of wishing you could fulfill all of you simultaneously causes for a disillusionment that leads to emotional uncertainty. It's quite hard trying to understand the complexity of satisfaction vs. the simplicity of contentment. Ego is a whisperer of desire & the spirit chases higher ground. Often they question why their mirrored existence is a distorted reflection.

Mind's Foreplay

I'm not squeaky clean. Even in my driven need to see my people elevate there's pockets of my mind that are dimly lit. They reserve space for the desired place where the untamed things play. Fantasy and imagery are constant entertainers in this gallery. Erotica of humanity but not everyone could understand the duality. The limits are scarce and the interest are pierced with yearnings that adorn the body. It's bejeweled with chemistry. It's all a foreplay in mentality.

Bizarre Senses - Loose Delirium

I am bizarre, by far. I am spiritually growing and losing grasp on reality's constructed normal-ism day by day. Yet, I am sexually intrigued and even physically engaged. I am in the balance between lust and expression. Yet through my moral compass I'm doing my absolute best to continue in spiritual gratitude and avoid triggers of depression, but I am expressive in nature. I have a sense of valor but it's buried behind my fear of self imposed danger. I am loosely honest, no hold to the fold. I am always thinking and often dreaming, but mostly I am distinctly & insanely seeking a way to have it all.

I want to be felt emotionally and relieved physically. I want to experience sexy, but also exchange Divine intuition. I want to laugh endlessly and express fearlessly. I want to pray and see manifestations of a miraculous Entity. I want to soar above restriction and feel free of conviction, but not to be careless in emotion but drenched in the peace of fully exposing. I just want a part of life written about. I want a tendency of intimacy that lives without complexity. I am bizarre by far. I have thoughts most refuse to endure. Here I am just a man yet somehow with a glimpse into Divine existence. Nonetheless, the urge to be human does not suppress. I am bizarre, and some believe I'm without stress. I guess I regress as I try to make sense of my lack of cohesiveness. I am layered and favored but mostly I'm bizarre, by far.

Sometimes I'm Just Thinking to Myself…

It's interesting how the mind is never blank but can feel so inexpressive. Is it the mind that lacks the expression or are the thoughts so layered that language doesn't quite do it the justice?

Be it as it may, deep within they stay and play hide and seek with knowledge. There's this space not fully diagnosed but it is somewhere between what used to be and the full onset of accepting what is supposed to be, but in the meantime we'll call this transition.

And I keep seeing the lights of the train as I post for most. A cluttered piece this soliloquy is, but a perfect replica of its original location before it manifested before you. If you've asked what does all of this mean? I guess you've reached the end; read it again & maybe you'll find something.

Floater

In the infinite abyss of this
We drift
With the possibility to give
What does not yet exist
It waits in the balance
For us to level the beam

To extract the dream
Into a land of new things
Don't let the words escape
As we wait
A time best to say
A massage too late
Pace
Trace
Face
Then relate the journey to those still traveling

Cult of Society

Oh how they watch & depict
Woven by ideals they worship it
Empty words to rhythmic beats
Adolescent bodies spread eagle in heat
Paying tithes to the social elite
Stunting is a habit
While debt is its receipt

Symbols of destruction
Blatant corruption
And we support it in the name of popularity

Ah, look at us...
We're all we can be
Shaved heads
Media fed
And Government assisted living dead

Who's behind the matrix we find
Rich zombies
Unspoken lies
Whoever or whatever they may be
They work for no better parts of me

Wisdom dwellers, it's easy to see
Look around you and pay attention
Pay attention very closely
Everything is & isn't what it seems
Uncanny paradox but true indeed
Take your stance
Lend a hand
Whisper knowledge to the next man

When they thought we couldn't
We showed we can

Fragmented Reality

> Get the fuck up & give a damn
> Rebels with a cause
> Niggas on pause
> But brilliance
> Ambition
> And recondition
> So we can conquer it all
> Death to the mentality of the
> Social Cult.

We

We, the majority, spend so much time discussing the minority.

We, the power, give so much energy to the system.

We, the dreamers, devote so many hours to sleep.

We, the gifted, let everyone define our boundaries.

We, the innovative, follow endless cycles of trends.

We are Thee & they are them. We could be so much greater than. We disguise & uphold their lies while life & time consistently pass us by. We fight battles that don't have life. Idle conversations condoning mediocrity, where's the ambition for a mission? Where are the geniuses of these men? We once were a body, and now we're fragmented. Chasing idols and bitches or men or them, whatever your thing is or might have been; right now hear my plea, lets release the me...let's turn this shit around flip it upside down and indestructibly become we.

Free The Vision

A Cleansing in the River
(الأردن)

For many years I never felt a transcendent love was necessary, nor possible, between me and a better half.
I felt the joy of friendship and lust of flesh were more than enough to suffice through life.
I hadn't seen any wrong with these things especially being that life was mine to mold and conquer.
Privately I felt deep within me was too much confusion and chaos that had lingered for as long as memories could serve me.
And the cleaning of my love-filled house would take as long as it took to build it.
It felt like a DIY project and no one should be willing to help.
Then I met her
She had become my glitch
The redirection to a misconception created long ago.
She gave me more than hope, which I never thought I was lacking, she revealed that my lack of acceptance was just a surface deception that hid a connection to someone more than me.
She made me desire something like a cliche.
The vibrant household & happy ending
She made me want to be more than I had grown accustomed to.
She was like a baptism in a love manifested
A cleansing in the river
A replica of Matthew 3:11
She was like a new language giving me the ability to communicate with many places foreign to me.
I was entrusted this glimpse of distinction.
I had to ask the Creator if this indeed was possible to be more than a vision.
Then just as blissful as it arrived it became disrupted.
The submitted prayer came with a ticket number that told me to wait until further notice.
In the meantime it was my duty to work on this old house of mine.
I had fallen somewhere between senseless faith, disillusion, & bitter.
Internally, I knew she was just a host of necessities later to be my

responsibility.
I love her, and she loves me, but words nor circumstances can force time to do what it must on its own.
We stand between our greeted glimpse and our distant forever.
I give her the space and give time the peace of working harmoniously.
I can only ask God to not allow a connection so beautiful to be a tease of vanity.

Marveling...

I sat by many days watching the sun's rays deliver growth over a place filled with creatures determined to destroy it. I marveled deeply at the light's consistency to shine independently of the agenda of individuals depravity of each other. I pondered upon the the work of the One who often got forgotten in the credits.

A forgiveness so strong that despite us who allowed our demons to become our reasons, we were granted a range so wide that we couldn't contain its size. Though they often tried.

Creatures so sure of themselves, yet never able to fully see all of their wealth. Can your eyes see the back of you? Can your ears hear the silence of your thoughts? Or are those illusions waiting to be chosen to manifest through you? Yet many only believe in what's in your view?

Take into notion that much exist beyond your ocean and our issues are a pinch of sand compared to all the lands. You are enough as you are, to become who you are meant to be. Don't confuse that to mean, that you should not change for the sake of embodying larger dreams.

The moon could never disgrace the sky just to survive but found balance living in unison despite their differences. One should have no desire to cohabit with a disease, so may we pray deathly vaccination upon all that which perpetuates greed. Like the rays of the sun lighting our days, too much heat burns the trees to make way. And even in those ashes life recycles giving way to a new order...so is life and we are its forester.

There's No Time

The concept of time is very vague, but felt to be so concrete. If we take off our frames of superiority and consider all that exist beyond us we would realize there is no time beyond our world of understanding. It is only here, on earth and by the accordance of humans, that time is believed to exist.

The world is apart of a symphony that's still being written. We are engulfed inside of the Uni-verse. We are submerged in outer space. Outer space is just as much home as the Earth is, and by the understanding of the universe time does not have measure, there is only existence. We create the measure of time based on our need to organize. For a moment let's suspend the idea we feel of time, and examine that days are the exact equivalent of hours, which also equals minutes, and ultimately builds to years. There is no time, there is only existence.

We live in a world of illusions. Once we release our ideals of when and how, we can accept the here and now. There is a "time" or moment for all things. Life is a host of moments, and only the Creator can conceptualize what will or could be. The Almighty Creator of all things. It's humbling when you realize that you're just a single note to this rhythmic orchestra. If all clocks stopped life would continue. Don't let the fear of lost or misguided time confuse you from the power in now. Thank God for all that is, because all is one and one is all. We live together, so ultimately we are One of the same. We share our air and sun if we can do that naturally, maybe someday/moment we'll see we can live as we began, as One.

The Blinds

Closing my blinds
I cut off my sight
Meditating on the visions that illuminate my mind
Futures unseen
A presence pristine
All praise to the Most High El Shaddai
King of all Royals
Creation is ours.
We see so much but these visions untouched
We build life & release with trust

Indemnify

v. – to guard or secure against anticipated loss; give security against

In this day of great redemption the power of restoration lies within the peace of forfeiting our disillusions.
The hindrance of correctness breeds a cycle of pseudo control. Life offers a placebo of contentment until growth comes to enhance all the understanding of what was.

A Spirit of Excellence has no room for that which fights to remain complacent. We are on a one way road to execution; whether that of our lives or our visions. In a desperate need to leave our fingerprints on time's tapestry we shower our nows with great passion. In hopes someone who comes behind us in the cycle of time, which may be perceived as the future, can pick up our fractional masterpiece re-solidify its loose ends with reinterpretations and allow those lost to be found again. In Love we say this, Amen.

Examine the Symphony

Music had been our soother during the times of great oppression. It had been our route to knowledge and code to freedom in the midst of deep despair. The humming tunes of slaves echoed through fields as the only glimpse of joy while blood callused hands and mangled bare feet worked forcefully to the bone with no signs of relief. It was a melody that carried us.

The profound and magnetic sounds of harmony sang courage into the body of those physically shackled. Now from your body to your mind they've refurbished the cattle. If music could heal or direct you to a road of relief, in reverse it can enslave and surely mislead.

So if you lend me your ears and rent me your heart, I'll feed you a truth to restore compassion to art. As once sang on the front lines of battle, we shall overcome, once we flee from the shadows. Music is universal and naturally your body shall move, but every dope beat ain't a dope tune. Be wise the lyrics and true the words, be conscious the message and question what is heard?

Don't Wait, Create.

Sitting in silence, I searched for the voice of reason. Stagnate in my position I waited for movement, or signs of its arrival. Then that voice I had been looking for spoke.

My blockage had been the fact that I was waiting. Although, I strongly believe there's a time to wait & stay still, there's also a time to move. Wait when you've done all you can & the control has escaped your hands. Our dreams should tire us in our reality. Our goals are to create something we don't see in the life given to us.

We are the plugs to this infinite source of power, but we have become so comfortable with using a surge protector to stop us from tapping all the way in, so we wait. We wait on someone else, we wait on contrived media, technology, or elitist to make a move so we can follow. Everyone wants to jump in a moving vehicle but no one wants to work the assembly line.

We are time stained walking memories. What's your legacy? I use writings & digital creativity to express what I do and don't see. Life is greater than us, and in all honesty we're all in a line moving toward death, but that's not morbid...that is truth. So in this line you can build monuments on your way to the end so others behind can learn, enjoy, grow, study, & be inspired to do the same making life a better existence or we can just wait until our number is called and leave purposelessly. Tomorrow is an illusion of yesterday, but today is only a temporary reality. Go create.

Accidental Genius

It was the many mistakes, submerged in the complete grace of God, that let me say today I am alive. It was the various hours of silence and struggle that pushed forward through the trouble that gives me proof to show that I am purposeful.

It was the discovery of the spirit that covers me that empowered me to write. I am an unbalanced ratio of insanity and brilliance. I am fighting for space in the world that's displaced by self-serving indulgence. I am guilty of it as well, but nonetheless my spirit prevails.

I stumbled into truth and took a reflection over my youth just to find proof of the genius I never knew. The genius that lives in me. The genius I found under siege by mediocrity. He's fighting his way through, and I've been told he wins with no doubt. So I sit and wait for the genius to make it out. His discovery was an accident, but thank God he's been found.

Do or Die

Let's discuss the unsaid
Let's address the living dead
The watchers & clockers
The speakers but lack of receivers
Let's discuss the "entertainers"
Let's focus on the retainers of a culture empowered
Why must we dumb down in order to turn up?
I feel like a revolutionary in the midst of a set up.
Coin-Tel
As in people for sell.
Given death by lethal ignorance
We must bridge the distance
We must analyze the lyrics
We must redefine our minds
We must rise.
Now here's the question,
Do or Die?

L.O.W.

The Land of Wasn't took many travelers in her grasp.
Abandoned by a shipwrecked boat named *"Couldn't"*
they yearned for rescue.
In this land was the destitute man with dreams and passions washed into the seas from the sands.
Time did never oblige
Yet thoughts of newness proved to be lies
As birds of desire flew over to feast on their lives.
Entrapped they learned survival by methods of enslavement
Keepers of the green passage gave them some
But never enough to call it due payment
Repeated and defeated their days played in loop
As they looked over the horizon of pain and resentment mesmerized and aloof.
Then in a gust of wind a savior blew in
Bringing opportunity of new visions.
They called him Action
A pure satisfaction to days that seemed to have no end.
A director He was
In an armor of love
He built ores out of determination
And a raft out of trust
Those who believed took a try at his relief
Set sail to see and found the island had been a mirage and not quite a destination.

1-3-15 | Reflections | 3:28 a.m.

When we are most silent we can hear the truth of our thoughts fighting the chaos of sensory overload. Our peace of mind is looking for its carved time in our hectic schedules of a constant go. So engulfed in our need to fill the space we often result to distractions for instant satisfaction, thus our human desires we revel in.

No love lost on behalf the "Boss" it's understood your journey is buffered with protection and direction to an outlet for understanding and reconciliation. How beautiful the joy to hear your voice express the concerns of your heart, then to sit back and watch the Art of the Greatest Creator to ever exist, as intricate details formulate then manifest. Never forsaken in this design we can't deny our finds of our Maker's traces of perpetual love all praises to the Great Divine.

Conversation with Lonely

I've been with you for as long as I can remember. Your silence has driven me to seek the sounds of temporary pleasures in an effort to feel...something.

I'm the only voice in our conversations and I don't know if you're the best I can do or all I know. I'm imprisoned in our routine and I feel so passionately yet inadequately understood.

I've become uncomfortably comfortable with this sense of continued nothingness but yet I digress. There's much confusion in this, and I have no one to blame.

I'm exhausted by you, Loneliness. I want to fill your position with a companion that at least has potential to be called by another name. Someone who cares enough about me to want to sooth my pains, forgive my days, & encourage my strengths.

Until then it's just me & you, loneliness...communicating through this pen.

Lust an Old Companion

I met lust in youth. A friend of comfort who gave me much to do. It was like an imaginary companion to loneliness, boredom, and excitement. We shared experiences that dare not to be repeated, but hope to never been forgotten.

A trickster it often is, just at climax I find I need more. Never enough and some times doesn't fully show up. There's a naked truth to be told & a sense of growth to behold. Here I am wanting more of greatness yet wrestling with this hoe, but we have developed an understanding that the world would turn cold.

In truth, my weakest moments were shared openly with this pseudo companion. I've lived low, but the adrenaline it released left me feeling high. If you ask any addict their closest confidants are those they can relate to without judgment. I guess that's not a connectivity exclusive to addicts, ultimately we're all looking for that transparency & unfiltered existence coupled with the assurance that when I look up from this minor stint of low and coldness they are still there to receive me. I've come a long way but have a long way to go. Nonetheless, the peace I seek is that my Creator still finds worthiness, love, and forgiveness to extend me.

Currently Thinking... Version 2:02 - 10.13.15

The thoughts running rampant through my mind whisper words of morality, but they battle the mortality of my desires. I've been told that these short burst of satisfaction, often deemed hard to release, hold no comparison to the fulfillment of the levels higher up.

But here I am, dick in hand, asking myself what's a man? In all the contemplating there's a silent stating, "Carve your visions into life's marble and stop pissing in the sand." I can't lie, with a pure reply, I find fear in not knowing the full me. Losing the shell of who I used to be. Really getting to know a brand new Free.

There's a sense of governing going on in this cerebral court. There's much imbalance to this trial. I'm so far from perfect, but God undoubtedly feels I'm worth it and I'm trying to fight the fears of having been so used to being a fuck up and finding my come up.

Well, these are the thoughts of the a.m.

Hypotheticals

I could do a thousand deeds
They'll remember the one I did wrong
I could stand in an abandoned building basement deep
Insecure echoes could still haunt my peace
I can wait for hours
And move too soon
I could hold my tongue and come off all wrong
I could worry about tomorrow
And never make it to the night
I could stand before man
And be hated for what's right
I could curse change
And never slow it down
I could argue my beliefs
And die together with my opposers

Fathoming: God Listen…

Lord,

I've kinda lost my way in this world, running in circles as the days unfurl. As they alienate the thinker and crucify the believer asking questions into the ether seems like an illusion of grandeur. My self induced imperfections have distanced me from the connection of greatness that too lives simultaneously within me. At a loss for sympathy I reached for empathy and found a symphony of creativity so bright and iridescent. I picked up a brush of action and painted a canvas of life with passion an unveiled a masterpiece no strife could ever fathom.

The Last Today

I held your fear in my hands and I removed it.
I took your words of concern and I soothed them.
I sat in silence with you and brought you peace.
Just like tomorrow, you had to wait on me.
You had to feel me in the power of today.
You had to believe that I would be of no delay.
You ask for my attention and the universe had to shift.
All without creating a cosmic rift.
The timing of life is so specific.
You think you have control
But one day you won't exist.
So everyone stop and take a selfie of this.

Let's hope it lives beyond the kids.
Let's hear our words meant with action.
God forgive us all of selfish satisfaction.
Allow the need for better to take control.
Give yourself the healing of truths told.
We are human and together we live.
One day as strangers
The next day like twins.
Day to day and hour to minute.
Life is what's happening and you just happen to be in it.
Hear me now, and with no doubt, if you want more have faith and know...that life has already worked out.
Be led on your path and ask God to direct.
Because tomorrow there is no guarantees except...

Today will never come back.

Attention Addict

Attention is a hell of a drug
Sometimes I go online for it
Sometimes I fight for it
Sometimes I cry for it
Sometimes I lay low and tell lies for it
Sometimes I see others and imagine me
Attention is at a high demand
But the seekers are at a low frequency
But truly let us not act
Attention is a feast
But sometimes I'm willing to take it as a snack
We all want someone to give us that thing we need
The attention of that lover
The attention that makes my mind & body release
Attention is the new currency
Fuck bankrupt
Attention is killing legacies
I'm not exempt
Shit
I'm really an observational hypocrite
I too lurk the corners
Wanting to be caressed
A double tap on the tip
Or the fondle of the breast
Baby this is a new game
Yet we're playing it like chess
I want attention when I want it
So let's make it convenient
Call me a chef because this attention is seasoned
I'm feeling gourmet
But just for today
Maybe tomorrow
I'll want solitude
Then that attention can't stay.

Words from Under the Covers - 2.5.16

I never wanted to be "alone". Not in that by myself self sense but more so that companionship. It's just everyone wanted the best friend. I didn't really experience the intimate. I'll take my responsibility, a lot of self denial and confusion lived in me...sometimes it still visits, you see?

I never felt ready, but mostly because I didn't know who would "get" me. The satisfaction in my attachments has a deep reach. Everyone can't get to the depth to feel how it can please...there's so much more to me.

I had to learn to just be. I had an addiction to wanting those who didn't, or don't, want me. I've demoted the addiction to recreational play. Don't get me wrong, I wrote the lyrics to this song. I just didn't know hitting the notes could take so long. I'm a man that enjoys two yards. I love the blossom of the flower but I also like to climb trees. So growing in a jungle almost felt like first nature to me. Anyway on this day, I smile because God's light is still growing me. Thankfully, I am nourished beyond my sight. There's still something beautiful in this soil. It seems to still have fruitful life. I don't write this with pity, nor is this a low moment feeling empty. It's just one of those times where things feel blossoming and true. So I say what I feel, and maybe someone will find it helpful.

Run, Run...

Running to the beat
Feeling ready to retreat
 As my heart race
My relapse is like a relay
 Moving in circles around the feel

Looking up thinking I'm further than I went
My body still paces
My mind still chases
Illusions with loose conclusions
 In the now, my lonely has tainted my desires
I'm searching for a leveled ground
Just when I think I found steadiness
I see it's just a plateau
 A mirage
 This is just the course I see
But believe you me...
I'm still climbing

Confessions - It is What It is

I like him & I like her
Not always the most comfortable scenario
But the truth isn't far
I've told them, and sometimes it's obvious
But shit baby I'm a loaded cannon
When the rod is stiff
Sometimes I'm turned up to the max
Other times I relax
I feel my body pulsate
When I haven't even reached the climax
They both do different things
Call this truth uncanny
But shit if you didn't know
There's a wild thing in me
I some times like to explore
I'm gaining control
Heaven knows
I'm still a work in progress
When I see them
I feel like fuck it let's lose the clothes
I'm going to do me
If they're open we can do we
First things first
Play it safely
I'm talking too much
It might be this rush
Whatever it is
I see a beauty in the two
I've realized pretending won't do.

Riding Through

The road to progress is often dark. Finding little light with each step, but yet, illuminated with visions of ideals and will. There's a tangled dance between sustain & maintain. I ride a road of need and desire. A fork in the road and I'm trying to go higher. There's much to be done and infinite to see…I just keep riding until the destination arrives in me.

Random Flowing - 4.26.16 - NYC Travels

In the darkness vibrated the rhythm of a prayer seeking peace suspended in time. Here was the formulation of the space between intuition and reality. The transition of the untouchable into full mortality, but due to its nature it forever stayed rooted in the endless cycle of the Creator. Nothing being new under the glow, this was the reincarnation of the old with a new view. Through its evolution excellence became obvious. The heart of life beat at the octave of possibilities. There is no lose there's only continue.

In Route to Sydney, circa. 8-4-16

As I cross the ocean moving back & forward in time I realize the peace of mind that comes with understanding. I looked at life from 40 thousand miles high and thought how small it all was. In the air, there is no care, no rush, nor competition of the elements. In all their uniqueness, they still exist harmoniously. It gave me gratitude to know the Creator of me also aligned my existence with all of this.

I sit in an airplane seat with an air-plain view. It feels like love, as the sun rises above the horizon. It feels like passion, as the clouds part to allow the rays in. Even the stubborn clouds were not a hindrance to the Sun's existence, more so needy to wanting it's light to shine on them just a little while longer before they shared it with the world. I saw it as a person who receives light from someone and doesn't want to let them go.

We, the commoners, are not the true enemies of the state. The state of harmony, the state of growth, the state of peace, it's those who allow the influence of the mainstream cultural identity to shape their mentality that falls victim to low living. The people at the top are scavengers and in a trickle, down effect, we eat their slaughter, which tends to be each other.

Once we see, our lives as elite their greatness will not be a privilege it will be a facade. We will become the valued and the pursue a life of more. Just as the sun lights the world, we will spread our light across nations when we no longer accept what we've been given.

Passing Shell

The architects of life
We built empires reflective of our minds
We communicated with the land
And mirrored the works of God's Hands
The manifestation of Creation
We're the Golden Anchor
Provided the ideas society holds on to
Nothing new
Just stolen & rebranded by a savage crew
This life is an illusion of thoughts made real
What do we owe ourselves
Nothing less than a Nation rebuilt
Our blood is recycled
From those who built pyramids...
The power never left it took on a new body
In a new man
So when you feeling broken, remember you can.

Diseases of Humanity

The body had become overrun by illness and disease that all the cells feeding off its source became affected. Then into the system, a cure was introduced, but the jealousy of the hierarchical festering structure saw this new hero on the block as a threat. All the strengths once possessed in the union of the cells had been destroyed by the vision of dissension administered by the disease to man. In this regard, we found divisiveness while the head swelled in its greed, while the body over-eats in a need to compensate for loss things. Nonetheless, nutrition was scarce. The cure, or hero, kept trying rebirthing itself through generations in hopes to spark a resignation from the powers that be…either through conscious understanding or a rebellious unity. The efforts seemed incomplete but the disease would do all it could to fully delete the trace of cure the hero brought into the space. What kinda system is this place?

———————————— *BREAK*

We find this to be common in the battle for humanity. Greed & division through political tension creates a weakness in the body of man. We see the commoners spewing perspectives as if they've sat in the privacy of the boardrooms that lead to the tombs of the hero's sent to spread cures to the world. In what realm does knowledge find itself dangerous & ignorance find itself celebrated? In what state do we see liberation as a term of selfishness? Those in control killed the will to rebel against the plagues they impart every time they euthanized the ones with a mission to reform. We've watched this illness take control time and time again but refuse to diagnose it to destroy it at the root. History is the pathology on how to remove.

The Onlookers

Go on, look the other way while the lines of the militia paint the streets in black & blue.

Debate the relevancy of life while the blood soaks into the memories of the mother's pain.

Justify the death while the casket lowers into the forgetfulness of the times.

Shake your head at those fed up with the way them in suits destroy the youth.

Like and share, while people stare as the heart stops beating in the undefended body.

Black, brown, and colored tip the scales of the rationale for the "Others" when they assert their worth in the land that their callous hands & hard, forced, & free work birthed.

Watch and wait at the formation of a police state where peace comes too late.

Uphold doctrine until the Black man challenges it's legitimacy by just attempting to be simply free.

This is the personification of hypocrisy.

From the waters of Flint, Michigan to the blood trails from Minnesota to Baton Rouge.

We stand under siege while the regime breaks the rules.

To what do we owe this disgrace?
America needs a new face because the spirits of the buried unjust are haunting it, in God's name.

They will not rest until their children are redeemed & victorious in the illustrious game.

No Limit—Humans

Humans are limited by their own creations, not by creation itself.

Humans are limited by their own existence, not by existence itself.

Humans are created in their own understanding but not in understanding itself.

If you could fathom the belief that something is greater than all that has ever been, or all that will ever be, then you will understand all that you are is just a blip in all possibility.

You are potential in its form of relativity.
You are potential in the form of now, not potential in the form of forever.

If we could understand that forever is an inconceivable measure, we would understand measure is not something we have the full capacity of.

We are not able to measure to the fullest extent that measurement itself can go.

We know that all measurement goes to the infinite extent of our life but within time, the future & the past, there are understandings that get lost in translation and long formats of communication because we are limited by our communications but not the communication itself.

We are limited by our own language, our own capacity to develop language, we are limited by our ability and forcing to grow.

We are limited by our own capacity to seek time, to be time, to be of time within time.

We are limited by our own need to define these things versus understanding that these things are simultaneously and infinitely and Divinely connected to one another and we are all a part of it.

Once we recognize the knowledge of its union then we would be able to tap into it and make it malleable for us to be able to be with it as well as a part of it.
Instead of explaining "it" as it being something necessary of definition versus being something worthy of a connection.

Going Through It – 9.1.16

I have to admit that I don't know shit. Like it's literally a fundamental deficit while I'm trying to win. I've felt myself running in circles waving at bystanders. People cheering me on like I've made progress, but all there is distress & looseness trying not to stop too long fearing regress.

Unfortunately, it didn't matter at all, because I wasn't out running my fear... I just exercised it. I feel like daily I don't know what, who, or where I am. Broken in my will, I've gotten less enthusiastic about feeling like "I can..." I have advice for so many, but my bank comes up empty. They claim to see the value, but I just feel doubtful.

God knows me by name & specifically by struggle. My life has constantly been lived in doubles. I want more but haven't mastered less. I want happiness and success, or vice versa, whatever the case I'm in a perpetual glitchy inertia. Out of a need for pacifying I've committed many sins... I pray God still sees me as worthy again.

This whole thing feels really fucked up and displeasing, but I'll work on believing. Even if in this second the answer isn't here, maybe in 5 minutes it will be clear. I'm trying to get back to anticipation. At the end of it all, this isn't just an empty conversation. I recognize some new aspects of an old depression... I don't need to relive those lessons. Maybe when a few projects are done I'll find peace. Maybe those accomplishments will set me free.

Bills still stack & accounts still lack. God be a come up in the form of a few thousand stacks. Of course without tragedy or destruction. Lord, I just need your loving. Having a hard time giving it to myself - please protect my mind, body, spirit, and health.

Retrograde, circa. 9-1-16

I felt it. For maybe one of the first times, I felt the spin. I felt a shifting within. My emotions redirected, and then I realized cosmically I was reflexive. I...I...I felt puzzled, not to cast off the truth of the struggle, and not to say that my lacks weren't lingering. It's just now I get the nature of the timely sensitivity. Some of what was in my head were also in the sky. You know, the whole "Universe is alive". And let me break it down, so it doesn't sound all "fake profound" or "pseudo-deep". Basically, you are what you seek. As above so below, inner thought becomes a physical and tangible show. We live in a living world, which lives in a living system, so its actions also create experiences. We would not be alive without it, so I was just becoming more cognizant.

If you've never heard of it, during a certain season the solar system is moving under different reasoning...and long story short it creates and/or influences different experiences. Before you rule it out, many believe in God without doubt...we would say "All works to the Glory of the Lord" but discredit the stars as if it is foreign to God's definition of "All". Anyway, I digress...but this awareness brought less stress. I began to understand it's just a rebirthing of an elevated man. So I do all I can, to create and rejuvenate my vision then see it expand. Through Mercury's Retrograde, I will...because I can.

True Story - circa. 9.4.16

I dreamed of a plane last night. I was going on a trip, but ironically the plane on the inside looked like a school bus. I was with my best friends and we were hype because after we landed we were going to Japan. I know this all seems very bizarre, but it was a legit dream so follow me if you can. The plane was kinda mediocre, and taking off but flying low. The plane was kinda rocky, so naturally, I was nervous about how it would make out. There was this fence in the distance, and I didn't know if the plane would be able to clear it. I remember in my dream I prayed and said: "God lift me, and protect this plane." Just as the words left my mouth the plane flew straight up, quickly but steadily too then immediately stabilized. Out of excitement, me and my friends celebrated. We talked about we couldn't believe how we were going to soon be going to Japan, we were in awe that we had done "it" or made "it". We started to drink, which for us is not uncommon...some on the plane weren't as excited. They kinda stuck out but as we landed they eventually disappeared...this dream became more obvious and less weird.

———————————— TRANSLATION

I was the plane, and my friends were my angels. The fence was my obstacles, and the rocky start was my process. It looked like a school bus because I was still learning, the prayer was, in fact, true and the take off was God's response. I can't speak to Japan, specifically, I have no real desire to be there...but I think it represents my urge to travel the world. It represents the foreign reward to my "dream". Those unhappy were my own emotions that I couldn't get past wanting to hang around but seeing they no longer fit. The landing was the securing of all I hoped, and now those other emotions left without hesitation.

I Know A Place

I'm on a hunt for the place where people are the freest. Where dancing is the native culture and laughter is how they speak. I want a place where the people are abundant and the problems are scarce. The place where there's nothing but harmonious rhythms in the air. A come one, come all type of call. Where we share in good vibes and energy that builds memories.

A place where children look upon it and feel nothing but happy. Where they peek through cracks at the adults gyrating to the bass of the stereo. I'm in high pursuit of an endless youth. That place where all the people are reformed by their wild stories & crazy experiences. Where the wisdom is best expressed through quotes & lyrics.

Nothing like the liberation found in the billows of smoke. There's drinks being passed and consumed. The view, whether clear or blurry, is of peace and sweat. The appetites are quenched with food being passed. I'm gazing and seeking this life. The place where everything always feels alright. So you can find me in the best party, conversations, and conventions...look for me in the middle where dancing is the only decision. I'm looking to be Free...no judgment or problems holding me. I'm looking to have this with you, let go & seek the openness of being full by being loose.

Point A to Point Be

There are times when it will feel like the dots just don't connect, or better yet you can't see the dots at all. There're times when you feel nothing but regret and everything is an inch from the fall.
There're times when you see all your problems and none of the solutions, or when everything that felt right, now just seems like a bunch of confusion. There're times where you know your talents and full capabilities, but money is the enemy of purpose because you always feel in debt and in need.

There're times when you're angry and feel completely let down. When you need direction or just a solid way out. Sometimes you look up asking for a break, and then your words feel misinterpreted as your faith shakes.

As hard as it feels, and undoubtedly seems. This is just a temporary moment like everything. Just as much as the money, that can come and go. Just as much as the love that now is a foe. Just like the family that has suddenly let you down, or like the happiness you thought you found. Life is lived in pieces every day is not the whole. So when things feel uneasy, you may bend but you will not break and you can not fold. The one thing that's constant is that you're in the middle of all of this. So it's YOU that's real, you are the plot-twist. These things exist because of the power of the Divine the beats in you. Always understand that when it's all done, you have already made it through. This moment is the past, present & the future all wrapped into one. Keep going and look up, here comes the sun.

American Quicksand

Many days I feel foreign to the world. I feel like a refugee in a land I do not understand. I feel as if I am no longer capable of being more than I am. I must pray for my faith because daily I feel the challenges of maintaining. I do not understand this lack of humanity, and I am losing compassion. I see so much work, that it's overwhelming to action. I am losing interest in the world. Very little excites me, I am feeling less optimistic. This hurts to say because deep within me I want to fairly play. I want to smile, joke, and laugh with a belief that this too shall pass. I believe in God, but damn "man" disappoints me.

Even myself, my lowness in the midst of my lonely. I want very little to do with the music or news. It feels like watching a simulation of a human. It feels like a repeat movie of a life once lived. It feels like I'm watching the conversion from man to reactors, lost in translation and destructive benefactors. I don't have much to say, this isn't depression it's probably feeling more numb than anything. Where do I go from here, and how do I see it all clear? What becomes an emotionless man with little in his hands? I don't have answers but I feel stuck in quicksand.

I Need This – I Just Want to Win.

It's imperative that I win. I feel like anything less is the true definition of sin. If I can't see my family elevated beyond the position we were put in then we have failed. I specifically will have never made the complete transition into manhood. All my visions would be just illusions and what would make me any different from someone who is considered crazy? I can't imagine a life full of "just enough" and false gratitude on being "happy you have the minimal". How could that ever be okay, when there is more than enough for everyone to have extra and it still is too much to consume?

I am scared shitless of running out of time. I'm racing a clock that has no minutes or hours. That acceptable space where dreams are still understandable to have. I am trying to see that you can be whatever you put your mind to. Is that too much to ask? Or should I raised children and tell them, don't waste your time only a select few make it any higher than ground. I don't want my children to see me like this. Somewhere stuck still trying to figure it out.

The world is under reform, that much we know. Yet, somewhere deep in me, I feel the right to have a say-so. I feel a need to be involved in the shifting and shaping. I feel the desire to own the Divine rights given to me. I sense there's more to life than just struggling. I feel the idea of adulthood can be redefined. I feel we can see the world and expand our minds. I feel there is something greater in creating than accepting. I just want to win. I need to win. I owe so many people who believe in me, including my future self.

Earth's Diamond

He came from the corner of the Earth
With the words of life in his mouth
He walked to the edge of the sea
Where the moon and the waves meet
Here is where all the prayers spread out
Found the existence of manifestation in the air
Vibrations of Love's worship surround his head
Building a mane from his hair
There was a cracking of an egg that birthed new life
A symphony of celebration rang from on High
The Stars bounced to the rhythm of his inner visions
Like a surgeon God carved his ideas in time
A see-section to the cosmic mind
Out flourished the inheritance of man
Wealth uncounted and blessings in hand
He rose surfing the waves of joy and grace
Smiles bloomed upon the Infinite's face
Now imparted he saw the horizon
Light beamed through his body
He, Earth's Diamond

Here Me Out: Under-Line

I have seen so much shit pass through my hands. I have watched opportunities ~~unfold~~ and life grow in different directions. No one can ever imagine where things will end ~~up~~. I understand that growing is a life ~~long~~ process. I know that much of the shit I ~~have~~ experienced could never be fully understood. Not because it's too deep but because it was ~~specifically~~ for me. I am no ~~saint~~. I am no ~~spiritual leader~~. I am a man trying to understand. Shit - I like to curse, drink, party, and explore…in the better and lonely times…often a whore. Yet, this is life and I'm getting it right. I am above ~~nothing~~ but the ground. I just have a loud ass mouth. Bear, and/or bare, with me, as I try to carve out some new shit from some old shit.

Fragmented Reality

Fragment | ˈfragmənt |
n. -
a small part broken or separated off something

Reality | rēˈalədē |
n. -
a thing that exists in fact, having previously only existed in one's mind

We don't live our lives in wholes, everything is evolving. Life is a one day at a time process. On some of those days, we get caught up feeling like everything is wrong, or like everything is perfect. We get caught up thinking we don't have enough, or not worthy of so much. Whatever it is we're only seeing it in pieces. How can you not expect to see something different? How can we get caught in moments that are so temporary they were meant to be forgotten. Sometimes we replay them so often, it becomes the addiction to the memory that makes us recycle the experience. I'm guilty.

These are just the moments, nothing is forever. That includes life. I try to make things work and work the things I make. I see opportunity, but that doesn't always translate to money. Again, these are just the moments. I know that it's a process to progress and this is something like a step to it. I call this Fragmented Reality because this is how life works. It comes into being in pieces, it leaves in phases, it changes in moments and settles over time.

If we look at the pieces sometimes we can see the picture in the puzzle. We put them together with our actions and develop it with decisions. It is not always the best and we are not always our best selves. That does not mean the picture isn't an artistic masterpiece. Ever make the perfect mistake? That's what these experiences and words represent to me. They also symbolize the circle of mind –

Visions → Experiences → Memories

I just want to be one of the dopest creators that life has touched.
Shit, I just want to be dope period.

A Letter From the Future

Free,

I appreciate what you've done for me. I appreciate your help and support. I appreciate the way you learned and the things you were taught. I appreciate the fact that you kept believing in yourself when you didn't have much to show. I'm glad you kept that idea in mind and didn't let anyone know. I'm glad you were able to make it beyond the struggles of feeling low. I'm glad we got to have that conversation even when no one else had hope. Bruh, we have really come a long way. Now look, you have more good things that are willing to stay.

I have to tell you, I know you did a lot of fucked up shit trying to get right. I know you gave interest to more than you needed, too, trying to feel alive. I'm not mad at any of that and respect you for it. They made for good stories and even enjoyment. We all have something that we hide or rather forget, so don't beat yourself up for being a grown ass kid. Everything has been blessed and we're happy now. No child learned to walk without falling down. Shit, it's nothing like being real and having seen the world. Even if it was in some low places, you were fishing for pearls.

It took a little time to realize you can't make everyone happy. I like that it wasn't too long because you were always authentic to yourself. Now we get to see the world, create films, books, meet people, and have art that none could have imagined. You're actually a Creative Director, and they're paying you more than you can count. They want to hear what you say and fuck those who don't. We made it kid a long way from Passaic, New Jersey. Your mom is happy with her gifts, and the family is proud.

Just remember you don't owe anyone anything, keep living out loud. It's ok to be great and analyze it sometimes. Never doubt whether or not that is for you, God gave us the sunshine. You will continue to have more, this is just me checking in. Everyone you felt you couldn't live without, look around. You're better without them. Life is not as hard as it seems, we're all capable enough to achieve. I'm just writing this letter to say, damn man, we've done some really dope things. Thank you.

Love,

- Free.

Free III
(3rd Time's the Charm)

I came into the world named under the generational name of my father. He insisted, like him and his father before him, I am called Free. Not by chance but by declaration. In all of the generations, including myself, each man had their deeply rooted struggles to becoming Free. Although this name had been given to each of us at birth, the guidelines and "how-to" was not provided. It wasn't until my young adulthood that I came to understand this. All the anger, confusion, or misguided perspectives fell off when it became my turn to take on the Free-challenge for myself.

When you are able to strip the world of titles, ranks, and affiliations you are able to see life a lot more clearly. You are able to understand the beauty in a man whose intellect surpassed his ability to effectively express it in a constructive way. You are able to appreciate the genius in survival through tough times, and an environment or society, not supportive of black genius in the 1950 & the 1960s. You are able to forgive absence on the account that it is not a true reflection of a lack of love but a battle between winning, elevating, and self-understanding. Every person and place has its own complexity, and our capacity to love until we grasp them is a true tale of strength.

With a wisdom unmatched built on street brilliance, self-reflection, mentorship, and Divine intervention I was raised not by the errors of my father and his before him, but the mission of healing passed to the next. With every generation that is called Free, I find each one becomes more liberated than the one before them. This in my belief is an inspiring place to be. To know up the lifeline, at least three generations back, was a visionary who understood the power of words. A person who knew that if you call someone something for long enough they will begin to become and believe it. We have been called Free since birth.

My father loves me unconditionally, and that is shown in immeasurable ways. If ever given the chance to pass this Free name along, I hope to see mine do it better than any of us. Until then, the 3rd time is the charm.

- Free III

From, Shank.

Sacrifice – n. • an act of giving up something valued for the sake of something else regarded as more important or worthy

My mother sacrificed for me. My mother gave her body, her time, her mind, and sleepless nights. My mother sacrificed her life for me, her money, her dreams, and even her being. She decided to never be the same not mentally, emotionally, or spiritually. She let me live from in her, to with her, and I would never leave her dreams or prayers. I am the product of sacrifice.

Internally, the blood and skin that is "I" was built from the inside-out. Now, I thank my father for his identity, tone, talent, & delivery. His stamp and immeasurable contribution...but a mother's nourishing breast and distress are priceless. Her inability to separate from the moment conception infiltrates can never be replaced. I have searched every language, connotation, and denomination - and still, I cannot find the word to define the absolute Divinity of motherhood but God's design- so I say thank you. Thank you for your life and your time...

My mother sacrificed for me. She gave her literal blood, sweat, and tears...so these words can be written here, and over the years I pray from my mouth to center of God's heart, priority, and ears that I will be able to pay you back with love, financial freedom, and success that is limitless. To you God, I'll give it my best. May greatness be forever awake, and peace always at rest in our lives. My mother, I am the living and breathing example of your sacrifice.

Thank you Ma.

Thank you for the support!

Free The Vision

ABOUT THE AUTHOR

Born under the name Freeman Warren III, Free The Vision is a Creative Director and Writer who expresses his artistic vision and voice through books, radio, visuals, conceptual art, and various other mediums. With a passion for people, love, growth, spirit, and adventure Free finds himself constantly moving through life on a mission to find the best experiences. As a Creative Director & producer, he is the liaison between vision and reality. As a writer, Free is the voice of a necessary thought, and as a visionary, he is the insight of a future made better.

Free writes for multiple digital publications, host & creative directs a podcast and also serves as the creative advisor to business start-ups. This is just beginning of Free The Vision's long and inspiring career and he is on an infinite rise to the top.

Wherever that might be.

Connect: @FreeTheVision

Free The Vision

Free The Vision

Made in the USA
Columbia, SC
31 March 2018